(1)

ANCIENT GREECE

Ancient Greece

CHARLES ALEXANDER ROBINSON, JR.
REVISED BY LORNA GREENBERG

A GROLIER COMPANY

A First Book | Revised Edition
FRANKLIN WATTS | 1984
New York | London | Toronto | Sydney

FRONTIS: THE ACROPOLIS, THE MOST FAMOUS MONUMENT OF
THE ANCIENT GREEK CIVILIZATION, RISES ABOVE MODERN ATHENS.

Maps by Vantage Art, Inc.

Cover photograph courtesy of
The Metropolitan Museum of Art, Rogers Fund, 1907.

Photographs courtesy of
Greek National Tourist Office: frontispiece, pp. 3, 16, 31, 37, 44;
Metropolitan Museum of Art: pp. 6 (Rogers Fund, 1941), 14
(Rogers Fund, 1914), 26 (Harris Brisbane Dick Fund, 1950), 32
(Fletcher Fund, 1959), 43 (Rogers Fund, 1913), 53 (Purchase, 1910, Funds from
various donors); Ron Greenburg: p. 11; American Numismatic Society:
p. 19; Peter Allen: pp. 23, 38; The Italian Cultural Institute: p. 54.

Library of Congress Cataloging in Publication Data

Robinson, Charles Alexander, 1900-1965.
Ancient Greece

(A First book)
Rev. ed. of: The first book of ancient Greece. 1960.
Bibliography: p.
Includes index.
Summary: Provides a history of ancient Greece, describing the people,
their myths, art, architecture, literature, philosophy, and daily life.
1. Greece—History—To 146 B.C.—Juvenile literature. [1. Greece—History
—To 146 B.C. 2. Civilization, Greek] I. Greenberg, Lorna. II. Title.
DF215.R634 1984   938   83-21572
ISBN 0-531-04727-X

CONTENTS

FOR MY GRANDCHILDREN

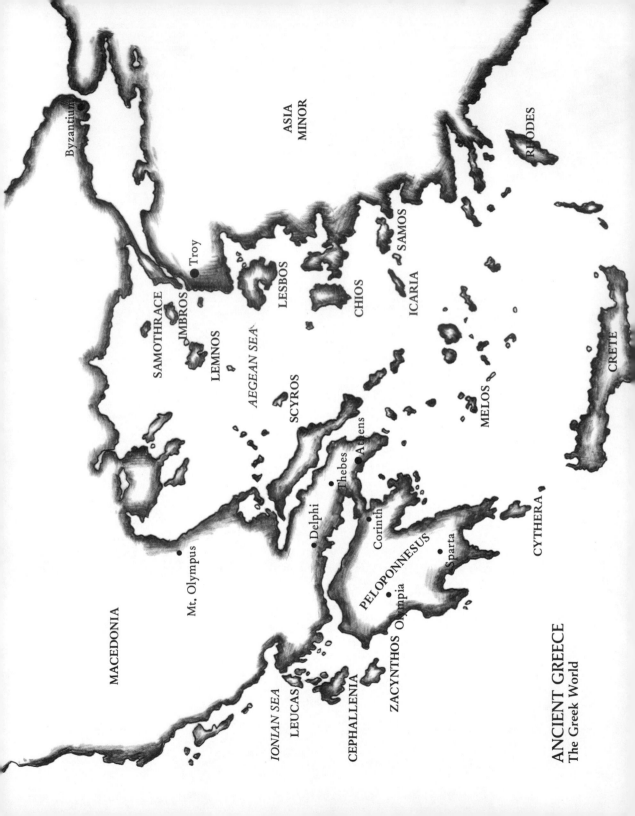

ASIA
MINOR

RHODES

Byzantium

SAMOS

Troy

SAMOTHRACE

IMBROS

LESBOS

CHIOS

ICARIA

LEMNOS

AEGEAN SEA

SCYROS

CRETE

MELOS

Athens

Thebes

CYTHERA

Delphi

Corinth

Mt. Olympus

Sparta

PELOPONNESUS

MACEDONIA

Olympia

ZACYNTHOS

CEPHALLENIA

IONIAN SEA

LEUCAS

ANCIENT GREECE
The Greek World

FROM THE LAND OF GREECE

In southeastern Europe, jutting into the Mediterranean Sea, is the mountainous peninsula called Greece. It is a small country—only 50,962 square miles (131,986 sq km) in area, about the size of New York State. Greece is a beautiful land. The brilliant sunshine often makes the mountains look purple. The long coast line is so broken that the deep blue sea seems to be everywhere. In the Aegean Sea, the part of the Mediterranean that lies east of Greece, there are many islands. The highest mountain in Greece is Mount Olympus, which rises 9,570 feet (2,917 m) above sea level. The Greeks of long ago believed that the immortal gods lived on Mount Olympus.

This is the region where, 2,500 years ago, an independent people created the first democracy in history. Around them, in other lands, absolute rulers had built empires and controlled the lives of many people. But in Greece the land was naturally divided into small districts by mountains or sea. So geography stood in the way of a central ruler. Small communities grew up in the many separate areas and on the islands. In the communities, each person was valued and thought of as an individual—not as a ruler's subject or as the servant of a god. This belief in the importance of the individual person led to the creation of what we call—from the Greek, *demokratia* (*demos*, the people; *kratos*, power)—democracy.

In addition to developing democracy, the Greeks' beliefs led them to value individual abilities and achievements. They produced beautiful art and literature. And they dared to investigate the physical world—to try to understand the nature of their world and the forces that shaped and controlled it. Thus they opened the way to science—mathematics, astronomy, engineering and more—by their faith that people could discover the truth by the use of their minds. Through their respect for the individual and the power of the individual's mind, they created one of the greatest civilizations in the history of the world.

People have lived in the region of Greece for at least forty thousand years. In the earliest days, small bands of people who lived by hunting and gathering their food roamed across the land. By 6000 B.C., these early people had begun to form settlements, and had learned to grow some of their food. Over the next three thousand years, the population grew and spread through the lands around the Aegean Sea. At times waves of newcomers moved into the region, bringing new ideas and skills. The people grew barley, wheat, peas, lentils, and other crops and raised sheep, goats, cattle, and a few other animals. They made simple pottery and baskets.

About 3000 B.C. the rate of progress began to increase. This was the beginning of the Bronze Age in Greece (3000–1200 B.C.). Historians divide early history into periods based on the materials the people of the time generally used for their tools and weapons—first stone, then copper, bronze, and iron. Over the course of this Bronze Age, two great civilizations developed in the Greek region, flourished for a time, and then died.

On the island of Crete a creative and spirited civilization grew up beginning about 3000 B.C. It is called the Minoan Civilization, after its legendary ruler, King Minos. It was a rich civilization of great palaces, marvelous paintings and pottery, and a form of writing (given the name Linear A) that we have not yet learned to read. By about 1450 B.C. the civilization had weakened, and the

Restored sections of the Minoan Palace of Knossos
on Crete, with beautiful paintings of vase-bearers,
demonstrate the creativity of this early civilization.

second great Bronze Age civilization, the Mycenaean, seems to have taken over Crete.

The Mycenaeans are the first people we call "Greek." They developed as the descendants of a great wave of people who swept down from the north into Greece sometime about 2200 B.C., and mixed with the people already there. These invaders spoke an early form of Greek. By about 1600 B.C. they had built a strong civilization with advanced skills and a written language we call Linear B. This script has been deciphered and shown to be an early form of Greek. The most important site was Mycenae, in the Peloponnesus, the southern part of the Greek peninsula. But by 1300 B.C. this civilization too had begun to decline. There was overpopulation, too little food, other internal problems and wars until, about 1200 B.C., the already crumbling civilization was hit by a huge invasion of a forceful, Greek-speaking tribe from the northwest, the Dorians. With this last great wave, the Mycenaeans fell, and the two glorious Bronze Age civilizations were gone.

The centuries that followed (from about 1200 or 1100 to 800 B.C.) are called the Dark Ages of Greece, for the richness and learning of the earlier civilizations had been destroyed. The people lived on a primitive level, and had little contact with the world outside Greece.

MYTHS AND HISTORY

Through the long centuries of the Dark Ages, traveling poets and storytellers kept alive some memory of the great Bronze Age civilizations by the legends they told. One legend tells of the Greek hero, Theseus, who sailed from Athens across the Aegean Sea southward to the island of Crete. There he slew a terrible monster with a bull's head and a human body called the Minotaur. The Minotaur was said to live in a huge underground stable called a labyrinth, full of twisting paths and a maze of tunnels where a person could get lost and never find the way out. Thousands of years later, beginning in 1900, a British archeologist, Sir Arthur Evans, excavated at Knossos in Crete, where Theseus was supposed to have slain the Minotaur. Instead of a labyrinth, Sir Arthur found a beautiful palace that had belonged to King Minos. It is several stories high and covers 6 acres (2.43 ha). On the walls are bright paintings of palace life and flowers and birds.

The most famous legends of the Bronze Age center on the story of the Trojan War. Troy was a city on the coast of Asia Minor. According to the story, Paris, son of the Trojan king Priam, went to visit Menelaus, king of Sparta in Greece. There he fell in love with Menelaus' wife, Helen, and carried her back to Troy.

The chieftains and warriors of Greece—Menelaus, Achilles, Ajax, Odysseus—banded together under Agamemnon, the

[5]

mighty king of Mycenae, to bring back "the most beautiful woman in the world," as Helen was called.

For ten long years the Greeks and Trojans fought outside the walls of Troy. The Greeks could not get inside the city, but neither could the Trojans drive them away. At last the Greeks defeated the Trojans by a trick. They built a huge, hollow wooden horse and left it outside the walls of Troy. Then they pretended to sail home.

When the Greeks left, the Trojans came out of their city to look at the strange animal more closely. Near it they found a single Greek soldier who told them that the horse was an offering to the goddess Athena. Believing that the horse would bring them luck, the Trojans decided to drag it inside their city. But the horse was so large that they had to tear down part of their walls in order to bring it in.

What the Trojans did not know was that some Greek warriors were hidden in the belly of the wooden horse. That night the warriors crept out and opened the city gates. Their companions who had pretended to sail away returned and rushed in to capture the city.

This was supposed to have happened in 1184 B.C., not long after the end of the Bronze Age. About four hundred years later—sometime about 800 B.C.—we believe a great Greek poet, Homer, took these legends of the Trojan War and created a long epic poem, the *Iliad*. The *Iliad* centers on the story of how Achilles, the best of Greek warriors, became angry and refused to leave his tent

Scenes from Greek myths were often illustrated on vases and other pottery. Here a fifth century B.C. artist has shown Theseus slaying the Minotaur.

until finally his dearest friend, Patroclus, was killed. Homer ended his poem with the death of Hector, the great Trojan hero, who was slain by Achilles.

The *Odyssey*, a second great epic, may have been composed by Homer. It tells how the wily Odysseus wandered for ten years on his way home to Ithaca from Troy. His faithful wife, Penelope, waited for him all that time. On his long way home Odysseus, or Ulysses, as the Romans later called him, had many fascinating adventures. Among the strange people he met were the enchantress Circe, who turned his companions into animals, and a one-eyed giant called Cyclops.

These are some of the legends about early Greece. Once they were looked upon as myths, without any background of historical fact. But Heinrich Schliemann changed that. He was a German-born businessman who spent many years of his life studying the places mentioned in the great poems of Homer. He believed that there had really been a war between the Greeks and Trojans. To prove it he set out, in 1870, to find and excavate the city of Troy. He was the first person to excavate layer by layer, and his success was very great. He proved that there had once been a city of Troy, and that there had really been a Bronze Age, too.

FROM THE DARK AGES TO A NEW AGE

The world Homer looked back at in the *Odyssey* and the *Iliad* was very different from his own world—the Greece of the Dark Ages, a period from about 1200 to 800 B.C., after the collapse of the Mycenaean civilization. In place of the impressive Mycenaean towns, there were only small, poor villages. Fine silver and gold work and pottery were replaced by simple pots. There was no knowledge of writing, for the system the Mycenaeans had developed from a Minoan script was lost. The Dorian invaders from the north had settled in, mixing with the population already there, and pushing some people out to Asia Minor.

But from this poor beginning, through the 400-year dark period, the framework for a new, even more magnificent civilization was created. A great deal happened in this shadowy time. In earlier days, many different languages had been used in the Aegean region. By the end of the Dark Ages, nearly all the people spoke some form of Greek. Families and clans became the centers of life, the most important social institutions. A new political system developed, to replace the old, king-ruled societies. This was the "polis," or city-state, where all citizens had rights and duties. Iron came into common use for tools and weapons. By the end of the period, a new system of writing had been created, based on an alphabet adapted from the Phoenicians. Greek legends and the

Homeric epic poems set a religious and moral tone, and even the beginnings of a Greek style in art appeared. Trade recovered and the population began to grow again.

So, by about 700 B.C., the people emerged from their Dark Ages, with a new Greek spirit for a new age.

The beginning of the seventh century B.C. marked the opening of a new era—the age of colonization, from about 700, or a little earlier, to 500 B.C. It was to be a time of growth in every area. The population in the Greek settlements around the Aegean Sea had become too large for the land to support; the land was too poor to provide enough food. Many Greeks sailed out to found new colonies. They settled on the shores of the Mediterranean, especially in Sicily and southern Italy, and the Black Sea, and in areas of northern Greece. In lands that were already settled by non-Greek people, they set up trading routes.

In moving out from Greece, the Greeks came into contact with different peoples and civilizations—Assyrians, Egyptians, Phoenicians, and others. They learned new ideas and skills, such as ways of working metals and making clay figures with molds. Most important, they were freed from old, narrow ways of thinking.

Wherever the Greeks settled, each new colony was set up as a polis, or city-state. The polis had developed from loose tribal beginnings in the Dark Ages. Every polis was a small, completely independent political unit, with its own constitution. All citizens of a polis were members of it; they had rights and duties and a part in its life. There were hundreds of the states spread throughout the Greek lands, each a small community, separated by mountains or the sea from neighbors.

At first, about 700 B.C., most of the city-states were led by kings or local nobles. In time different forms of government appeared. Sparta was ruled by kings, later by an oligarchy (government by a few—usually, the wealthy). It developed into a military state, with all areas of life strictly organized. This may have

At Paestum in southern Italy, as throughout the ancient world, the Greeks established colonies and spread their art and culture. These majestic temples date from about the sixth century B.C.

happened because Sparta had many helots—serfs, or peasants, who were subjects of the Spartan state. They were bound to the soil and were under the rule of the owner of the land they worked. In 640 B.C. the helots, who outnumbered the citizens, rebelled. After about twenty years of warfare, the Spartans put down the revolt and changed their government to insure that the helots would never again be strong enough to rebel. In Sparta, service to the state, courage, and discipline were greatly valued.

Athens was first ruled by kings, then oligarchs, then tyrants—rulers who took power for themselves, with no legal or family claim to it. It then became the world's earliest democracy. The people were the rulers of the state and each citizen had a part in the state's government. Corinth was ruled by tyrants and then by an aristocracy—"the best," as the nobles were called. Syracuse, in Sicily, was at different periods an aristocracy, a tyranny and a democracy.

MANY STATES—ONE PEOPLE

While the city-states developed different forms of government, the civilization throughout Greece was pretty much the same. The citizens' loyalty was to their own polis, but more and more they came to think of themselves as one people. They had a growing sense of being "Greek." From the Homeric poems they took a common history. They shared a language and alphabet, and a common desire for independence and self-rule. Ceremonies, festivals and contests that drew Greek citizens from all the far-flung colonies also strengthened their sense of being one people.

One of the most important Greek festivals was the Olympic Games, held at Olympia, in the Peloponnesus. The games began as religious festivals where contests of strength and skill were held to honor the gods. From 776 B.C., regular games were held every four years at Olympia, in honor of Zeus, the father of the gods. Athletes from all over the Greek world competed in running, jumping, throwing the javelin and discus, chariot races, wrestling, and boxing. Winners were awarded crowns of olive leaves, and were highly honored when they returned to their home states. Contests were also held at Delphi, Corinth, and Nemea, but the games at Olympia were the most famous. Athletics were such an important part of Greek life that many cities had

gymnasiums, and held local contests in their own stadiums. At Sparta, girls too entered athletic competitions.

At Delphi there was a religious shrine for all the Greeks. Here, on a slope of Mount Parnassus, was the Delphic Oracle, where human beings could ask the gods for advice on private or public matters. The oracle at Delphi, the most famous Greek oracle, was sacred to Apollo—the protector from evil, and god of Greek civilization. Questions or requests for advice were given to a human priestess, called the Pythia, who entered Apollo's temple to receive the answer of the god. She pronounced it to priests, who then rephrased it, usually in verse, and presented it to the advice-seekers.

The oracles often gave good, sound, everyday advice. The Delphic Oracle urged the Greeks to colonize the Mediterranean, which would relieve overcrowding at home. It also urged them to free their slaves. Sometimes an oracle looked into the future. When this happened, the priests tried to phrase the answers very carefully, so that they could be taken to mean various things.

When Croesus, a wealthy king in Asia Minor, was threatened by the Persians, he sent to Delphi for a prophecy. He was told that a great empire would fall. He thought this referred to the Persian Empire, but it was his own that fell.

Another time, when the Persians were about to invade Greece, the Athenians asked the oracle what to do. They were told to put their faith "in their wooden walls." Some thought this meant the wooden palisade around the Acropolis. These people

Athletic competitions, such as this footrace scene pictured on a sixth century B.C. vase, were an important part of Greek life.

[15]

were killed when the Persians attacked and took the Acropolis. Others said the oracle meant the wooden bottoms of their ships, and it was through their navy that the Athenians won.

Sharing common gods and legends also helped make the Greeks feel like one people. The most important and powerful gods—the twelve who dwelt on Mount Olympus—were sacred to nearly all the people. They were: Zeus, the sky god and father of gods and humankind; Hera, his sister-wife who protected marriage; Poseidon, god of the sea; Demeter, goddess of agriculture; Athena, goddess of arts and wisdom; the twins Apollo, god of civilization and Artemis, goddess of the wild; Ares, god of war; Aphrodite, goddess of love; the clever Hermes, messenger and protector of travelers; lame Hephaestus, smith to the gods; and Dionysus, god of wine and the drama.

Each city-state also claimed one god as its own. Their special or patron deity at Athens was Athena; at Corinth, it was Aphrodite. There were festivals in honor of the god and, in return, the patron god protected the city and its people.

Ceremonies and rituals were performed in temples throughout the Greek city-states. This fine round temple to Athena is at Delphi.

[17]

THE RISE OF ATHENS

When Greece emerged from its Dark Ages (after 800 B.C.), Athens was just one of many city-states—and some, Sparta, Corinth, Miletus, and others, were much more powerful and important. But in the early sixth century B.C., things began to change rapidly.

Athens was then ruled by an aristocracy, and there was a great deal of unrest and unhappiness among the people. The poorer farmers were oppressed. If they fell into debt and could not repay their loans, they were sold into slavery. In 594 B.C. the Athenians, anxious for changes, elected a poet and reformer named Solon to be archon (a ruling official) and law-giver. Solon attacked the social and economic problems of Athens. His first emergency measures included cancelling all agricultural debts and mortgages. He stopped the selling of people into slavery for debt, and set free many who had been sold. He led Athens toward democracy by giving the citizens some voice in the government. He divided the citizens of Athens into four classes based on their income, rather than on their birth. Only members of the three upper classes could hold offices; but all citizens could attend the assembly which elected government officials. He established a people's court.

Solon also took important steps to improve economic conditions. He set out to change Athens from a farming community to

About 600 B.C., the Greeks began to use coins, and many
city-states minted their own money. Shown here are:
(A) a silver coin from Syracuse showing a chariot with a
flying Victory crowning the horses as a symbol of Syracuse's
victories at the games at Olympia; (B) a silver coin from
Corinth with the figure of Pegasus, the legendary winged
horse; (C) a gold coin from Macedonia, bearing the head of
Apollo crowned with a laurel wreath; (D) a popular silver coin
of Athens, showing an owl, the sacred bird of Athena.

one that could grow rich and important by manufacturing. Athens had fine natural resources—the marble of Mount Pentelicus, silver from the mines of Laurium, and the wonderful clay in the Plain of Attica, which was used for the beautiful vases which were soon being exported throughout the Aegean region.

To make Athens a manufacturing center, Solon had to bring in craftsworkers from outside the state. Athens did not have enough potters and vase-painters, or enough artisans to make shields, jewelry and other items. To persuade skilled workers to come to Athens, Solon offered them citizenship. This was a bold new idea, for in Ancient Greece, you had to be born in a state to be a citizen of it. Solon convinced the Athenians to allow foreigners to settle in Athens and become citizens.

After Solon's time, Athens was ruled by a series of tyrants. Then, about 508 B.C., another gifted reformer gained power—Cleisthenes. Cleisthenes was to be one of the most important shapers of Athenian democracy. He reorganized the government and gave every free citizen, even those with no property, the right to speak and vote in the assembly. The people gained greater political freedom, including freedom of speech and the right to equal treatment before the law.

From this time Athens was, in essence, a democracy. The people were the rulers of the state and each citizen had a part in its government. With this new freedom and power, the Athenians were firmly on the path to becoming the most important city-state in the Greek world.

THE PERSIAN WARS

While Athens and the other Greek city-states were growing in strength, another civilization was also gaining power. To the east, from Asia Minor to India for a distance of 2,700 miles (4,344 km), stretched the mighty Persian Empire. Unlike the independent Greek city-states, the Persian Empire was one large unit—controlled by one absolute ruler, the king. Each Persian king tried to leave his son an even larger empire than the one he had inherited from his father.

In the sixth century B.C., the Persians under Cyrus the Great conquered the Greek cities in Asia Minor. The great Persian ruler, Darius, turned his eyes to Greece itself. In 490 B.C., he sent his fleet across the Aegean Sea from Asia Minor to attack Athens.

The Athenians, begging for help, sent their best long-distance runner to Sparta. But the Spartans did not want to risk a battle with the mighty Persians and claimed they had to finish their ceremonies of the new moon. And so, when the Persians landed on the Plain of Marathon about 20 miles (32 km) from Athens, they faced the Athenian general Miltiades and his Athenian troops, with just a small force from the nearby state of Plataea. Nevertheless, the Greeks beat the Persians decisively in a bloody battle and, for the moment, Greece was saved.

The full, long story of the Persian invasions was recorded by the first great historian, Herodotus, who lived from about 484 to 425 B.C. He has become known as the "Father of History."

The spirits of the Athenians were high after their marvelous defeat of the Persians at Marathon. But they did little to prepare for the possibility of another invasion. Finally, the able and forceful general Themistocles convinced them to use a rich, new find of silver to finance the building of a fleet of ships. And, when news of Persian activity began to reach Greece, a small group of city-states—including Athens and Sparta—met at Corinth and agreed that they would fight.

These actions were barely in time, for in 480 B.C. the new king of Persia, Xerxes I, began to move against Greece. He assembled a huge force of more than 180,000 men and over 600 ships and set out northward by land and sea along the north coast of the Aegean, and then on south toward Athens. Leonidas, the brave Spartan king, tried to stop Xerxes at the narrow pass of Thermopylae in central Greece. He and all the soldiers with him were killed after a heroic stand. The Persians moved on to take Athens and burn the Acropolis. The Athenians were evacuated by their fleet. Then Themistocles tricked the Persians into the narrow channel near the island of Salamis. There the Greek fleet surrounded the Persians and crushed them. In the spring of 479 B.C., the remains of the Persian army were destroyed too.

At last the threat of a Persian attack was over. A band of fewer than thirty Greek city-states, fighting together for the first time, had beaten the mighty Persian empire. The Greeks were full of new confidence and energy; sure of themselves and their ability to shape the future as they wished.

No one could be absolutely sure, however, that the Persians would never attack again. So in the winter of 478 B.C., Athens invited many of the other Greek city-states to meet on the sacred island of Delos, under the protection of Apollo. There they agreed to form a league—called the Delian League—against Persia. The

On the small island of Delos, sacred birthplace of the god Apollo, five stone lions guard the temple ruins.

Greeks in Asia Minor who had just been freed from Persian control were anxious to join. So were the Greeks of the Aegean Islands, since a new Persian fleet could pick them off, one by one. Sparta, however, chose to go its own way and did not join the new league.

Each member was to contribute ships—if it was rich enough—or else money to pay for ships which Athens would build. A trusted Athenian statesman called Aristides the Just was chosen to decide each state's fair share. Every state was to have an equal voice.

In the next thirty years the Delian League—under the leadership of the Athenian general Cimon—was successful in pushing the Persians out of the Aegean, and even fought them in Egypt. But from the start, Athens was the dominant state. Nearly all the others found it easier to supply money rather than ships. So Athens was soon in control of the league's treasury and had it moved from Delos to Athens. Athens punished states that refused to join, or tried to leave the league. Athens began to manage member-states' affairs, and stationed soldiers inside their lands. The states were forced to use Athenian coins and the Athenian system of weights and measures. Gradually, what had begun as a voluntary league had turned into a empire, under the rule of Athens.

PERICLES AND ATHENIAN DEMOCRACY

By the mid-fifth century B.C., Athens was the center of Greek civilization and dominated every aspect of the Greek world. The Athenians had created a thriving democractic state at home, and a large and wealthy empire abroad. It was the center of trade, of culture and learning, and of political, economic, and military control—except over the strong, rival city-state of Sparta. This was the "Golden Age" in Athens—from the defeat of the Persians in 479 B.C. until 431 B.C., when a new war began. Through this period, the history of Greece focuses on Athens.

The person most responsible for making Athens great was a statesman named Pericles. He was elected one of the chief magistrates at Athens nearly every year from 461 B.C. until his death in 429 B.C. During his many years in office he pursued his belief that the people should rule themselves and should have the benefit of an empire—democracy in Athens, and imperialism abroad. He was such a stong guiding force that this period of Greek history is often called the Periclean Age.

Athens was one of the largest Greek states. It covered about 1,000 square miles (2,590 sq km). The city was 5 miles (8 km) from the sea, with a 20-foot (6.1 m) high stone fortification wall around it. Since an enemy army might try to starve the city into surrender,

Pericles ordered two long stone walls to be built—to connect Athens with its harbor, Piraeus. The walls were 4 miles (6.5 km) long, and more than 500 feet (152.4 m) apart. As long as the Athenian fleet ruled the Aegean sea, food could be landed at Piraeus, even in wartime, and brought to Athens between the long walls.

Athens had a population of about 250,000 people. Most were citizens and their families. Some were foreigners who lived in Athens for business reasons, but did not seek citizenship. There were also about 20,000 slaves, for slavery was widespread throughout the ancient world. In earlier periods of Greek history, defeated enemies and debtors were forced into slavery. After 594 B.C. a law forbade the selling of debtors into slavery. Slave dealers began to appear, who bought prisoners of war and then sold them for a profit. People captured by pirates, unwanted children, and barbarians (to the Greeks, barbarian meant non-Greek) were made slaves.

Slaves worked for the state as government clerks or public laborers, or worked for private employers—in agriculture or the mines, in a manufacturing industry, or in a household. The slaves could save part of their earnings and hope to someday buy their freedom. Some slaves had responsibilities; the Athenian police were state slaves that had been brought in from Scythia, in what is today southern Russia.

In the time of Pericles, trade and business flourished. The standard of living rose. Beautiful temples, such as the Parthenon, were built on the hill of Athens called the Acropolis. The state supported religious, dramatic, and other festivals.

The powerful goddess Athena,
represented in a fifth century B.C.
statuette, flying her sacred owl,
held all of Athens in her care.

There have been few moments in history as great as the Periclean Age. Life was exciting, creative, and inventive. Ordinary Athenian citizens could take an active, direct part in public affairs. The people had the responsibility of running Athens and the empire of which Athens was the proud capital. To do this, the Athenian citizens met in their Assembly, the Ekklesia, once every ten days. The Assembly was held in a natural hillside amphitheater on a slope called the Pnyx, opposite the Acropolis. This was the foundation of the Athenian democracy. All free male citizens over the age of eighteen were members; all could attend the meetings, speak from the speaker's platform, make motions, and vote. What the people decided at the Assembly became the law.

Every year five hundred citizens were chosen by lot from the Assembly to make up the Council, the Boule. The job of the Council was to attend to the business of the state between meetings of the Assembly, and to prepare proposals to bring before the Assembly at its next meeting. No one could serve in the Council for longer than two years. About 451 B.C. Pericles ordered that members of the Council and jurors be paid, so that the poor could serve without suffering.

The chief executive officials of Athens were the Ten Generals. This was the board to which Pericles was elected year after year. The Ten Generals were more than military leaders. They carried out the decisions of the Council and Assembly. They met foreign envoys and supervised the many officials of the state—such as those in charge of collecting taxes and repairing the ships.

The right to equal justice and a fair trial by other citizens is an important part of democracy. Every year the Athenians selected by lots a panel of 6,000 jurors, from among those who volunteered to serve. Juries of 201 or more citizens were then chosen—again by lots, to prevent bribery—for each trial. People had to speak for themselves in a trial, but they could hire a speechwriter to prepare a speech. The jury was in effect a committee of the people, and its decision was final.

The Athenian democracy was not perfect. The existence of slavery was one obvious flaw. Women were denied many rights—including the right to vote. But the citizens of Athens in the days of Pericles felt they helped run the government and had a stake in its future. With freedom and opportunity went responsibility. The Athenians who helped run their government carried home a feeling of responsibility for their own and others' welfare that benefited not only government, but every aspect of Athenian life.

LIFE IN PERICLEAN ATHENS

The main social unit in Athens in the fifth century B.C. was the family. And here, as in nearly every area of life, men dominated. The family was a close and devoted unit, ruled firmly by the father. Women's lives were controlled by their husbands. Respectable women rarely appeared in public, except at funerals, weddings, and festivals. The woman's job, the Greeks believed, was running the home and raising the children.

Girls received little education, beyond spinning, weaving, and other home crafts and, perhaps, basic reading and writing. Boys were luckier. The state required parents to educate their sons, but there were no public schools. So most boys, from about age six to fourteen, were taught in small groups, by educated Greek slaves or hired teachers. The sons of wealthy parents might then continue studying with a tutor. The boys learned reading and writing, and some mathematics. Music and athletics were very important; as were the poems of Homer. In these poems boys learned about the heroes of the past, and about the gods. An ambitious Athenian boy might also study rhetoric, or public speaking, for this skill might further his chances of being elected to a public office. But before he could aim at that goal, he would have to serve for two years of military training after reaching his eighteenth birthday.

[30]

Stories of the gods were studied and provided a
common history for the Greeks. This sculpture depicts
Zeus, king of the gods, carrying off young Ganymede
to Mount Olympus, to be cupbearer for the gods.

The sunny climate of Athens made living outdoors especially pleasant. For that reason, Athenian men looked on a dwelling more as a house than a home. They left their houses early in the morning for work or relaxation.

On most days, the average Athenian man worked at his job. Providing food for his family was his chief concern. He might have been a farmer, cultivating vineyards and wheat fields, or looking after olive trees. Perhaps he was a skilled worker, making articles such as cups, mirrors, or sandals in a small shop or factory. Some Athenians were shepherds and fishermen. Others worked in trade or commerce.

The typical Athenian house stood beside a narrow, crooked street. There were no ground-floor windows facing the street, just a door. Inside, life centered around a courtyard. This was open to the sky and was planted with flowers and bushes. Along the sides, a tiled roof held up by columns gave protection from rain and sun. It was in the colonnade, or open courtyard, that Athenians visited and talked, and there was nothing they enjoyed so much. The sleeping and living rooms were arranged around the courtyard. Occasionally there was a second story, which was reached by a ladder.

Furniture was expensive, and people had little beyond simple chairs and tables. Wealthier families had decorated chests for storage, a dining room with couches on which diners could recline, and chairs with cushions. Every house had a shrine to Hestia, goddess of the earth, and the family gods.

Greek sculpture, as in this marble tombstone carving from the fourth century B.C., shows the simple, graceful clothing and furniture styles.

The houses were built of sun-dried bricks, which washed away little by little in the rain. When a house collapsed, as Greek houses often did, everything in it would be buried. Then, instead of carting away the debris, the Athenian leveled it off and built another house on top of it. Over the years, a mound would slowly rise—a sure sign to a modern archeologist where to excavate to find relics of Ancient Greece.

On an ordinary day, the average Athenian man rose early and put on his knee-length woolen garment, called a chiton. Women usually wore ankle-length versions of the chiton. On cool days, a cloak, or himation, might be added. The wealthy sometimes had clothes made of linen. After a small breakfast of coarse bread dipped in wine, the average citizen might go off to the market at the Agora, the central meeting place of the city, before beginning the workday. The citizen might have tucked a small coin into his mouth, for Greek clothes had no pockets.

The market was a large, bustling area, with special sections for each kind of item shoppers might want. Bronze bowls could be found at the metal-workers' booths, fish at the fish market, oil at the oil market. Barber shops offered a place to collect news and gossip; water clocks and sundials told the time. The Agora was also the civic center of the city. Much of the official business of Athens, such as the meetings of the Council and the worship of the gods, took place there. The most important buildings of Athens—the Council House, the law courts, the mint, arsenal, and library, as well as a music hall, temples, and colonnades—were all in the Agora.

After a light lunch at home, the Athenian might spend some time in the afternoon at a gymnasium, where he wrestled, boxed, and ran. And almost always, there was some time for serious discussions with other citizens.

Except when there were guests, the Athenian families ate dinner together. The meal usually included olives, vegetables, such as peas, beans, onions, cabbage, or turnips, and often fish, cheese, bread, apples or figs, honey for sweetening, and wine mixed with water. Meat was too expensive for most people. The food was cooked, by a slave or the woman of the house, over a wood or charcoal fire. Olive oil was used in cooking and as fuel for lamps.

If an Athenian man wished to entertain friends, he usually invited them home for dinner in the evening. During dinner, the men leaned back on couches. As soon as the meal was finished, the guests decided on a topic to be discussed. Plato, the philosopher, says his teacher, Socrates, was particularly welcome at dinner parties because he was able to talk so sensibly.

ART AND ARCHITECTURE

Athens at the beginning of the Periclean age had little of the magnificence we expect of the heart of a great and prosperous empire. The Persians had completely destroyed the Acropolis in 480 B.C. So Pericles set out to make Athens a glorious city. He sought the best architects, sculptors, and artists of the time, and persuaded the Assembly to provide money for building. He also used funds that the members of the Delian League had given Athens to pay for ships. When he was criticized for this, he said that as long as Athens defended the League members, it could use the money as it wished.

Atop the Acropolis—the rocky hill that rises 300 feet (91.4 m) above the Agora and the homes of the Athenians—Pericles planned a splendid grouping of marble temples. The central temple was the Parthenon, built in 447–438 B.C., to honor the patron deity of Athens, Athena the Virgin (in Greek, "Athena Parthenos").

Ictinus was the major architect of the Parthenon. Callicrates assisted him. Phidias was its sculptor, and the person Pericles appointed as the general supervisor of all the new buildings planned for the Acropolis. He was perhaps the greatest sculptor of the fifth century B.C.

The Parthenon, like other Greek temples, was actually a structure built to protect a statue of the patron god or goddess.

[36]

The Parthenon, a splendid Doric temple,
crowns the Acropolis of Athens.

Another temple atop the Acropolis is the
Erectheum, an Ionic structure. It is famous for
these figures of women (carytids) who bear
on their heads the roof of its small south porch.

Phidias made a majestic, gold-plated 30-foot- (9-m-) high figure of Athena to stand inside the temple. Ceremonies were held outside the temple, at an altar. The temple was very large, about 228 feet (69.5 m) long, 101 feet (30.8 m) wide, and 65 feet (19.8 m) high. There were 17 columns along the sides; 8 at each end.

The Parthenon was built of marble, brought in from the quarries of Mount Pentelicus. This marble contains a good deal of iron. With the passing of time, the marble has taken on a golden glow from the iron content.

Greek architects invented three styles or "orders" of architecture: Doric, Ionic, and Corinthian. These names refer to different kinds of columns and other details or decorations. The Parthenon represents the Doric order of architecture. Many of the details of Greek structures were painted. Red, blue, yellow, and green were popular colors.

Greek architects had learned that from a distance, straight lines look as if they are curved. The architects planned carefully to correct this optical illusion. Every line was slightly curved, so that it would *look* straight. All the columns were built to lean slightly toward each other. Every horizontal line—every step or foundation—was "crowned." It rose slightly in the center. If you were at the Parthenon you could test this by placing a book on the corner of a step. If you then walked to the other end and bent down to the step, you would not be able to see the book. The center of the step is crowned; it is higher than the corners, and would block your view.

Sculptors worked closely with the architects to plan the decoration of the temple. Phidias designed sculptures to fill the triangular spaces at the ends of the roof (the pediments), to fill the spaces above the columns, and for other places in the temple. Today many of the Parthenon sculptures are in the British Museum in London. They were taken there in the nineteenth century, when Greece belonged to Turkey, by Lord Elgin, the British ambassador to Turkey.

The sculptures in the east pediment—over the main entrance—show the birth of Athena. According to legend, Athena sprang fully armed from the forehead of Zeus. The sculptures in the west pediment show the contest between Athena and Poseidon over which would be chosen the patron god of Athens. The people of Athens chose Athena, after she gave them the gift of the olive tree.

These great sculptures are "in the round"—they are fully carved and separate from the background. Other sculptures on the Parthenon are in "relief"—that is, they rise from the background of the blocks from which they are carved. The sculptures in relief form a frieze, or procession. They show the best young men of Athens on horseback at the time of a great August festival. Other young men and women are seen bringing animals to the sacrifice and various offerings to Athena.

The Parthenon and the other temples, with their many sculptures of gods and idealized human beings, tell us a great deal about the people of ancient Athens. We see what they admired and held up as ideals. The Athenians, like other Greeks, were devoted to their state and its gods. Therefore, the Parthenon glorified both state and gods. It was a monument to patriotism and to religion as well.

A period such as Periclean Athens produced many other great artists. A fellow citizen of Phidias was Myron. He is famous for his statue the *Discus Thrower*, which shows a young athlete in a split second of rest. This statue is a fine piece of art, and also reminds us of the importance Greeks placed on competitive sports and healthy bodies.

SOPHOCLES AND THE DRAMA

T he Athenians had many festivals throughout the year—athletic, religious, and civil. Many were put on by the state itself, and the most creative and talented people of Athens and other Greek city-states contributed to them.
Two major drama festivals were held every year in Athens. They were religious ceremonies and everyone was encouraged to attend: women, the poor (who might have had their entrance fees returned to them), children, prisoners (released from jail for the event), government officials, shopkeepers, and bankers—for all business was halted during the festival.

The festival in the early spring was the most important. It lasted about a week, because there were several processions and dances by groups, and a large number of dramas, both tragic and comic, were performed. The center for all this was the theater of Dionysus in Athens. Dionysus was the god of wine and vegetation, of new birth and gladness, and of the theater.

The theater of Dionysus was on the south slope of the Acropolis. It was open to the sky. The auditorium had stone seats and held about eighteen thousand persons. At the bottom was a circular area, called the orchestra, and here all the action took place. Beyond the orchestra was a long building which served as background. The building was called "skene" in Greek, from which we get our word "scene."

The plays were produced at a time of religious celebration. For that reason, an altar sacred to Dionysus was placed in the center of the orchestra. On the steps of the altar sat the chorus, for there was much singing and dancing in a Greek play.

The performers were of two kinds. There were three professional actors who played the various roles. (If a play had more than three characters, the actors played more than one part.) The actors, men for both the male and female roles, were paid by the state. They wore masks to show their characters and moods. The masks sometimes had mouths shaped like megaphones, though Greek theaters had very good acoustics.

The rest of the performers, twelve to fifteen men, made up the chorus. They both sang and danced. The chorus consisted of amateurs and was paid by a wealthy citizen who was appointed as producer by the state. At the end of the week judges awarded prizes to the best producer, the best actor, and the best dramatist. So the spirit of the festival was competitive, as well as religious.

The audience gathered at the theater not long after dawn on the first day of the festival. They saw a series of three tragedies by one dramatist. During the next two days, two other dramatists presented three tragedies apiece. Comedies were also performed.

Greek tragedies were nearly always concerned with the relationship between human beings and their gods. The stories were taken from legends of the heroic age, or Homeric poems, or from historical events. From this starting point, they explored the nature of humanity, and the question of the individual's worth and responsibility. The dramatists were, in a sense, the teachers of Athens. The three greatest tragic dramatists of the fifth century B.C. were Sophocles, Aeschylus, and Euripides.

Sophocles (496–406 B.C.), the son of a prosperous Athenian arms maker, was known to have written 123 plays. Only 7 have survived. He represents the Greek ideal that we must be both thinking and active people. In 443 B.C. Pericles appointed Sopho-

To portray different characters, Greek actors
wore padded costumes and grotesque masks,
as shown in this gallery of clay figures of
actors dressed for their roles.

cles chief treasurer of the Athenian Empire. Three years later, he served as a general in a war. In his dramas, this man of action was chiefly interested in what effect experience had upon a person's character and soul.

Oedipus the King is thought to be Sophocles's greatest play. It was based on a legend familiar to the Greeks since the time of Homer. Laius and Jocasta, the king and queen of the ancient city of Thebes in central Greece, were told by an oracle that a son born to them would murder his father and marry his mother. Terrified by this awful prophecy the parents gave their young son, Oedipus, to a slave, with orders that the child be left to die on a rocky mountainside. But the boy was rescued and brought up as the son of the king of Corinth, ignorant of his true background.

Years later, the oracle at Delphi repeated the prophecy to Oedipus himself. To avoid his fate, Oedipus vowed not to return to Corinth and the house of the man he believed to be his father. He set out for Thebes instead, but on the road met an elderly man in a chariot. After an argument about the right of way, Oedipus slew him. Without knowing it, Oedipus had killed his father.

At Thebes, Oedipus found a terrible plague blanketing the city. An oracle had said the plague would last until someone solved the riddle of the Sphinx: "What is it that walks on four legs in the morning, two at midday, and three in the evening?" Oedipus guessed it was a human being, who crawls early in life, later walks upright, and may use a cane in old age.

The sphinx fell over, and the plague disappeared. In joy and gratitude, the Thebans made Oedipus their king. And then he married Jocasta, the widow of the late king, not knowing she was his mother.

At the hillside theater at Delphi, the round orchestra and the foundation of the "skene" can still be seen.

By the end of the play, the truth has been revealed. Jocasta has killed herself, and Oedipus has torn out his eyes. Oedipus, while headstrong, acts nobly. Sophocles's audience was stirred by sympathy and fear at this tragedy of a person who is powerless in the face of forces greater than himself.

Aeschylus (525–456 B.C.) was a bold and dramatic poet whose tragedies were concerned with moral questions. They seek reasons for the laws of the universe. Only seven of his plays survive, including *The Oresteia,* a group of three plays that tell of the fate of the royal house of Agamemnon: *Prometheus Bound, The Persians,* and *Seven Against Thebes.*

Euripides (480?–405 B.C.) wrote plays of fierce criticism, and attacked many of the Athenians' attitudes—such as their treatment of women—and beliefs. *The Trojan Women, Medea,* and *Electra* are some of his best-known plays.

The only comic poet whose works have survived was Aristophanes (445?–380? B.C.). He wrote inventive, spirited comedies that ridiculed public figures, other playwrights, and even the gods. *The Birds* is a fantasy of an ideal kingdom; *The Frogs* attacks Euripides, while *The Clouds* makes the philosopher Socrates its victim.

PHILOSOPHY AND HISTORY

Even before the time of Pericles, the Greeks had been interested in science, although they could not carry their scientific studies very far because they lacked precise instruments. But with the rise of democracy and its ideals of human equality, the ordinary person had become important. It was natural that Periclean Athens should turn to the study of the nature of humanity itself.

Socrates (470–399 B.C.) was an example of the new attitude, of the new interest in humankind. He was a poor Athenian, full of loyalty and love for his country and its citizens. He loyally performed his duties as a soldier and as a member of the Assembly.

Socrates was "a lover of wisdom," a philosopher. In his pursuit of knowledge, he spent long hours thinking. He wanted to discover the truth. He particularly wanted to know what people meant by god and the immortality of the soul, by beauty and justice and democracy and their opposites. He tried to find out what is the best way for people to live and behave.

It seemed to Socrates that the gods were everywhere and knew everything. As he looked at the world, he felt that the world had been made for human beings. He said that there was a grand design visible, which could only be due to the wisdom of the gods, or as he preferred to say, to God. Socrates reasoned that since people are capable of good, God must have made them. Therefore, he added, the best of human practices and societies are the most god-fearing.

Socrates was forever moving through Athens, often going where the crowds were the thickest. His method was to stop people and ask questions. When he was given an answer, he asked another question and so on. He pretended ignorance on all things himself. But he kept asking more questions and soon forced his audience to recognize their ignorance. This was the first step to wisdom. He then gave his own definitions of such things as courage and beauty.

The Athenians eventually put Socrates on trial for his life. They said he encouraged young people to revolt against the state and the ancient gods. The charges were false, but the Athenians had recently lost a long war with Sparta and were tired. They were tired, too, of a person who was forever asking questions and seeking the truth. Socrates was condemned to death. While in prison, he had the chance to escape, but would not break the law. When a friend asked him how he wished to be buried, he replied that they could put his body anywhere, but they could never catch his immortal soul. As was the custom in Athens, his jailer brought him a cup of poison hemlock. Socrates took it from the weeping jailer's hands, drank it, and died.

Socrates left no writings. We learn about him from his pupils, the most famous of whom was the Athenian philosopher Plato (c. 427–347 B.C.). At the age of twenty, Plato joined Socrates's circle of followers and soon became one of the most important of them. After Socrates died, Plato wrote an account of his trial and death. His *Apology*, as it is called, presents the actual scene in the courtroom and is a glorification of the philosopher's life.

Later, Plato opened a school, "the Academy," where he taught a great many educated men and some women through the course of forty years. He also wrote dramatic works on philosophy. These are called "Dialogues," because in each work various people join in discussing a particular topic. The main speaker is always Plato's revered master, Socrates. Probably the most important dialogue Plato wrote is the *Republic,* in which Socrates discusses the ideal state—its educational, social, and political aspects.

Plato had a fine, creative mind. He led his students and readers to think hard about the topic under discussion. His most famous pupil was the philosopher Aristotle (384–322 B.C.). Aristotle, instead of asking questions, gave knowledge. He wrote a great deal on philosophy and politics. He also studied physics, astronomy, psychology and physiology, and zoology and botany, and founded a school in Athens. Throughout ancient times and even later, people referred to Aristotle's works and studies as if they were the final word on a subject.

Socrates, Plato, Aristotle, and many other bold, original thinkers of Ancient Greece were an important force in the rise of this civilization. It reached great heights because these people and other Athenians insisted on challenging anything they wished. They created new ways of thinking about the world of human beings and nature, and about life itself.

As Periclean Athens produced great philosophers, dramatists, and artists, we would expect that it would produce great historians as well. But instead of looking to the past, the historians emphasized the events of their own time. It was their own world that drew their interest.

The greatest Greek historian, Thucydides (460?–400? B.C.), chose to write of the long war between Athens and Sparta that raged during his lifetime. It was called the Peloponnesian War (431–404 B.C.), because the chief enemies of Athens—Sparta and Corinth—were located in southern Greece, in the Peloponnesus. The war ended with the surrender of Athens.

Like other citizens of Periclean Athens, Thucydides was both a writer and a person of action. He was a general in the war for a short time, but was exiled for failing in a mission. He then devoted himself to writing the history of the war. Thucydides is considered a great historian because of his careful reporting and because he was absolutely fair in his work. He loved Athens, his native state, but he did not hesitate to criticize it.

Thucydides traveled through Greece during the war, observing and questioning people on both sides. Beyond describing the course of the war, he aimed at uncovering the causes behind the war—the forces at work beneath the events he could see. He believed the war was caused by the other Greek city-states' fear of Athens. As Athens became an ever-larger power—as its empire grew—the other states feared they would loose their independence and be swallowed up. Since the time when Athens had taken control of the Delian League, or even earlier, Sparta had distrusted Athens. And the Periclean belief in democracy at home and a wealthy empire abroad, had made Athens seem even more dangerous. Also, Athenian democracy stood as a challenge to states governed by aristocracies or kings. Athens represented something new, and many people feared it.

As the war went on, Thucydides studied its cruelties and its effects on human values and behavior. And he was shocked when his own city of Athens adopted the policy that "Might Makes Right."

Pericles died in 429 B.C., early in the course of the war. A great plague had broken out in Athens, causing the death of as much as 20 percent of the population—including, perhaps, Pericles. He was followed by poor leaders. The people were persuaded to send an expedition across the Mediterranean Sea to try to conquer the powerful rival city-state of Syracuse, on the island of Sicily. The whole expedition, ships and men, were destroyed.

When, at last, the war ended, Athens surrendered and gave up its empire. It was the end, too, of the extraordinary fifth century B.C.

For the next thirty years (404–371 B.C.) Sparta tried to take control of the city-states of Greece. But it was a time of constant unrest and strife. In 371 B.C., Sparta was defeated by Thebes and this state then tried in vain to rule Greece. By 362 B.C. all the major states of Greece were exhausted.

PHILIP AND ALEXANDER THE GREAT

The greatest weakness of the ancient Greeks may have been their unwillingness to unite, to stop all their wars among themselves. From the earliest days of the city-states through the early fourth century, B.C., they wore each other down by frequent conflicts. At last they were united—but it was done *for* them by a conqueror from the kingdom of Macedonia in northern Greece.

In 359 B.C. the ambitious Philip II became king of the large but weak kingdom to the north of Greece. He quickly unified the tribes in his own region and set out to expand his realm. He conquered barbarian tribes and then turned against Greece. The great orator Demosthenes (384–322 B.C.) tried to alert the Athenians to this new danger, and to persuade them to unite with the other Greek states against Philip. When open war came, the Thebans and Athenians did cooperate at the battle of Chaeronea in 338 B.C., but Philip was victorious. In 337 B.C. Philip created a league of Greek city-states under Macedonian leadership. The independent city-states were now under his control.

In 336 B.C. Philip was assassinated, and his twenty-year-old son Alexander became king.

Alexander (356–323 B.C.) completed the conquest of Greece. He then marched east against the Persian Empire. He had about 30,000 infantry and 5,000 cavalry, whereas the mighty Persian

A carved gemstone from the third century B.C.
shows the head of Alexander the Great,
wearing the headdress of Herakles.

At the battle of Issus, Alexander the Great
defeated the Persians. This Roman mosaic
copy of a Greek painting shows the Persians
in retreat, under their leader Darius III
in the chariot at the center.

Empire had armies of 100,000 men and more. But Alexander was a courageous and extremely gifted military leader and never lost a battle. He led his men on a 22,000-mile (35,398-km) march, as far as India, and then back, but at Babylon, in Mesopotamia, he died of a fever, when he was not yet thirty-three years old.

Because of Alexander's conquests, the new, large world east of Greece now took on one civilization—Greek. Or rather, the various peoples in it—the Egyptians, Syrians, and others—kept their own ways and added Greek civilization as a sort of common bond. For example, even though Jesus and his disciples spoke a Semitic language, Aramaic, at home, the New Testament was written in Greek, so that everyone might understand it.

The new world, after Alexander's time, was made up of large kingdoms, not city-states. The most important of these was Egypt. The capital was Alexandria, which Alexander had founded and named for himself.

Alexandria grew to have a population of a million persons. It became a busy, prosperous city. Great scholars and scientists worked in its libraries and museums. Some of them studied and wrote about Homer and the Greek dramatists. Euclid (323–285 B.C.) wrote a book on geometry that is so clear that little improvement has ever been made on it.

Archimedes (287–212 B.C.), another scientist, discovered, as he was stepping into his bath one day, the relationship between weight and displacement of water—the principle of specific gravity, as it is called. He was said to have been so excited that he ran through the streets naked, crying, "Eureka, I have found it."

Perhaps the greatest Greek scientist was the astronomer Aristarchus (about the third century B.C.). His estimate of the length of the year was only seven minutes and sixteen seconds too short. He believed that the earth goes around the sun. This is known as the heliocentric theory. Most people did not want to believe that our planet was not the center of things, so they kept on believing in the geocentric theory, that the sun goes around the earth.

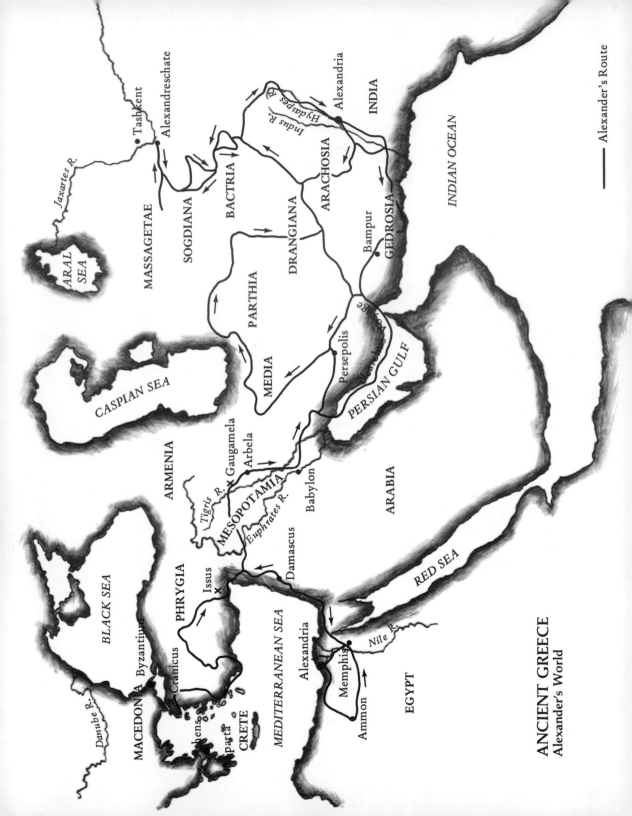

—— Alexander's Route

Tashkent

Alexandreschate

ARAL
SEA

Jaxartes R.

MASSAGETAE

SOGDIANA

BACTRIA

Indus R.

Hydaspes R.

Alexandria

INDIA

INDIAN OCEAN

DRANGIANA

ARACHOSIA

Bampur

GEDROSIA

PARTHIA

CASPIAN SEA

MEDIA

Persepolis

Nearchus Voyage

PERSIAN GULF

ARMENIA

Tigris R.

Gaugamela

Arbela

MESOPOTAMIA

Babylon

Euphrates R.

ARABIA

Damascus

RED SEA

BLACK SEA

Byzantium

PHRYGIA

Issus

Granicus

MEDITERRANEAN SEA

Alexandria

Nile R.

MACEDONIA

Athens

Sparta

CRETE

Memphis

Ammon

EGYPT

Danube R.

ANCIENT GREECE
Alexander's World

THE LEGACY OF GREECE

The new world that Alexander opened up to the Greeks and their civilization lasted for three hundred years. Then Rome, the great power from the west, in Italy, conquered it, and the ancient world was united in the Roman Empire.

The Romans adopted a good deal of Greek civilization, just as the Egyptians and Syrians had done. Since much of modern Europe—such as England, France, and Italy—was carved out of the Roman Empire after it fell, the civilization of the Greeks, as well as the Romans, has been passed on to us.

Perhaps the most important gift we have inherited from ancient Greece is the belief in the importance and worth of the individual. We also believe, as the Greeks did, that we should seek the truth and be guided by it. We should be warned by Greek history that war often leads to disaster, but that unity can produce peace and prosperity.

Much of Greek art and architecture is a joy to look at. Greek drama, philosophy, and other literature tell us about humankind and the meaning of life. But most important of all is the Greek idea of democracy, the belief that all people should be free to govern themselves.

WORDS FROM THE GREEKS

Amnesia. Loss of memory. From the Greek *amnesia*: *a* (not) plus *mnasthia* (to remember).

Alphabet. The letters of a language, arranged in order. From the Greek *alphabetos*: *alpha* plus *beta,* the first two letters of the Greek alphabet.

Bicycle. A two-wheeled vehicle. From the Greek *bi* (two) plus *kyklos* (wheel).

Crocodile. An aquatic reptile. From the Greek *krokodeilos*: *kroke* (gravel, pebbles) plus *drilos* (worm); worm of the pebbles.

Drama. A play. From the Greek *dran* (to do or act); deed or action on the stage.

Geometry. A branch of mathematics. From the Greek *geometrikos*: *geo* (earth) plus *metrein* (to measure); to measure land.

Herculean. Tremendously difficult to accomplish. From the Greek *Hercules,* the hero who performed difficult and dangerous tasks.

Hippopotamus. A large, African mammal that lives chiefly in water. From the Greek *hippopotamos*: *hippo* (horse) plus *potamos* (river); a water horse.

Metropolis. A major or capital city. From the Greek *meter* (mother) plus *polis* (city); the mother city.

Monarch. A sole ruler or emperor. From the Greek *monarkhes*: *mono* (sole or one) plus *arkhes* (first in time or rank); one who rules alone.

Museum. A place where works of artistic, scientific, or historical value are stored and exhibited. From the Greek *mouseion*; a temple of the Muses, the nine spirits who presided over learning and the arts.

Octopus. An eight-tentacled marine mollusk. From the Greek *oktopous*: *okto* (eight) plus *pous* (foot).

Planet. A celestial body. From the Greek *planetes* (wandering), *planetes asteres* (wandering stars).

Rhinoceros. A large, thick skinned mammal with one or two horns on its snout. From the Greek *rhinokeros*: *rhino* (nose) plus *keros* (horn); nose-horned.

Skeleton. The bone structure of a body. From the Greek *skeletos*, *skelein* (to dry up); a dried-up body.

Theater. A building or place for the presentation of performances. From the Greek *theatron*: *thea* (a sight), *theorein* (to look at).

Telephone. An instrument that transmits voice signals. From the Greek *tele* (far) plus *phone* (sound); sound far away.

FOR FURTHER READING

Asimov, Isaac: *The Greeks: A Great Adventure.* Boston: Houghton Mifflin, 1965.

Bowra, C.M. *Classical Greece.* New York: Time-Life Books, 1965.

Downey, Glanville. *Stories from Herodutus.* New York: E.P. Dutton, 1965.

Graves, Robert. *Greek Gods and Heroes.* New York: Doubleday & Co., 1960.

Homer. *The Iliad.* Retold by Barbara Leonie Picard. New York: Oxford University Press, 1960.

_____.*The Odyssey.* Retold by Barbara Leonie Picard. New York: Oxford University Press, 1952.

Levi, Peter. *Atlas of the Greek World.* New York: Facts on File, 1980.

Quennell, Marjorie, and Charles H. *Everyday Things in Ancient Greece.* Revised by Kathleen Freeman. New York: G. P. Putnam's Sons, 1954.

Ruskin, Ariane, and Batterberry, Michael. *Greek and Roman Art.* New York: McGraw-Hill Book Co., 1969.

INDEX

J 938 R 1984
Robinson, Charles A.
Ancient Greece / Rev., 2nd
ed. -- $8.90

DATE DUE		
JAN 31 '95		
MAR 16 '96		
APR 23 '96		
MAY 11 '96		
JUL 02 '96		
NOV 27 '96		
OCT 7 '97		
NOV - 7 1998		
MAR 31 1999		